101 WRITING PROMPTS

FOR GRADES 3-5

BOOKS FOR YOUNG WRITERS FROM RED WOLF PRESS:

Story Starters:

101 Story Starters for Little Kids by Maisy Day
101 Story Starters for Kids by Dena McMurdie
101 Story Starters for Teens by Maisy Day

Writing Prompts:

101 Writing Prompts for Middle School by Mark Trevor
101 Writing Prompts for Grades 3-5 by Mark Trevor

101 WRITING PROMPTS FOR GRADES 3-5

by
Mark
Trevor

RED WOLF
PRESS

RED WOLF PRESS

To contact the publisher about permissions, send an email to dmcmurdie@redwolfpress.com.

ISBN: 978-1-955731-08-9

Published by Red Wolf Press.

Interior design and cover design by Dena McMurdie.

Cover art by yusufdemirci, jannystockphoto, and MisterElements.

First printing, December 2023.

IMAGE CREDITS:
Front cover: all images depositphotos—background, hands, pencil, wood grain: yusufdemirci, doodles: MisterElements, post-it note: jannystockphoto.
Back cover: all images depositphotos—woodgrain, plant, pencil, post-it notes, paper clips: yusufdemirci, doodle: MisterElements.
Interior: All images depositphotos. **Page 5:** cat: marumayfay, **8:** lightbulb: anfisa_focusova, **9:** pencils: somjaicindy@gmail.com, **10, 15, 27, 62, 101:** banner, streamers: Teploleta, **11, 13, 16-17, 19, 40-41, 43, 45, 49, 100, 103-104, 106, 108-110:** emojis: Aratehortua, **21, 23, 25:** lion family: Aratehortua, **22, 26, 28:** BFF doodle: Aliasching, **24, 29:** Happy family traveling by car, Family picnic outdoors: Katerina_Dav, **30, 34, 44, 47, 92:** zookeeper with parrot, roller coaster ride, girl reading, boy in tree house, dog with megaphone, supercat flying, spy kid: ronleishman **48:** old scroll: frescomovie, **50:** space ship and stars: ksenya_savva, **51, 55, 59:** backpack: ksenya_savva, **52, 54, 56:** camper: Qilli, **58:** sports balls icons: Vikeriya, **60-61, 63, 65, 66-67:** hands reaching for the stars: Curvabezier, **69:** time machine: memoangeles, **70, 72-73, 75, 78-79:** book doodle: blue67, **71:** boat: Kopirin, **77:** tickets: musiyaka2@ukr.net, **80, 82, 84-85, 87, 89:** boy and girl with megaphone: freudjon, **81:** cat and dog best friends: AlonaS1984, **88:** video game controller: lhfgraphics, **90-91, 93-95, 97:** thinking emoji: catalyststuff, **99:** cute faces: Aratehortua, **102:** group of children whispering: artpustovit.gmail.com

TABLE OF CONTENTS

FOR TEACHERS & PARENTS

Welcome! As a Language Arts teacher with nearly twenty-five years of classroom experience, I know how challenging it can be to engage students in writing assignments. It can be even more difficult for elementary school students who need more real-world experience and background knowledge. That's why I created this book of fun writing prompts—to help spark their imaginations and get words on the page.

This book contains over 100 engaging writing and drawing prompts for students in grades 3-5. These prompts will encourage students to use their vivid imaginations and produce thoughtful, interesting responses. You'll find plenty of topics children like to write about—themselves, family, friends, pets, and a few that allow their imaginations to run wild.

You can use these prompts in various ways: assignments, warm-ups, journal entries, creative writing exercises, persuasive writing, and more!

I am honored that you chose my book, and I hope it will be a valuable resource.

MARK TREVOR

FOR YOUNG WRITERS

Writing can be hard, but it becomes easier and more enjoyable with practice.

Here are a few tips that will help:

1. Brainstorm ideas.

Before you start writing, brainstorm for a few minutes. Make a list of your thoughts and ideas to help you get organized.

2. Start with a "hook."

A hook is usually the first sentence of a story or essay. Writers use them to catch the reader's attention and make them want to keep reading.

For informational or nonfiction writing, begin with a clear topic sentence that states your main idea. (Tip: Try using part of the prompt in your topic sentence!)

3. Don't forget the details.

Use details and examples to make your writing more exciting.

Instead of:	Try adding some details:
The dog was happy to see me.	The dog sat up and wagged his tail when he saw me.
Chicken nuggets are good.	Chicken nuggets are crispy, juicy, and very tasty. They are my favorite food.

4. Review and edit.

Always review your work and see if something needs fixing or changing. Pay attention to spelling, punctuation, and capitalization. Make sure each sentence starts with a capital letter and ends with a punctuation mark.

5. Get feedback.

Show your writing to someone: a friend, classmate, teacher, or parent. Ask them how you can make your writing better. (This step is optional, but it's a great way to share your ideas and talents with others!)

BONUS TIPS FOR ASPIRING AUTHORS

Do you love writing and want to get better at it? I have two more tips for you:

1. Read. Read. Read!

Read as much as you can. The best writers spend plenty of time reading. Books, articles, news, webcomics—it doesn't matter what you read as long as you do plenty of it. Reading improves your vocabulary, helps you think of new ideas, and makes you a better student.

2. Practice. Practice. Practice!

Write often. The more you write, the better you will get at it. Here are some ways you can practice writing and have fun at the same time:

- Keep a journal
- Write song lyrics or poems
- Create a comic strip
- Write a story
- Write old-fashioned letters to family and friends.

LET'S GET STARTED!

ALL ABOUT ME

What is your favorite holiday? Christmas? Ramadan? Chinese New Year? Diwali? Something else?

Pick a holiday and tell us why it is your favorite. Describe what you and your family do to celebrate it.

ALL ABOUT ME

Who are you a huge fan of? A famous athlete? Someone from history? A singer, dancer, or actor? Pick a person you admire and explain why you like them. Be sure to tell about some of their achievements.

_____

_____

_____

_____

_____

_____

_____

_____

_____

_____

_____

_____

_____

_____

_____

_____

_____

_____

_____

_____

_____

_____

ALL ABOUT ME

What is your favorite game to play? Is it a sport like soccer? Or maybe you like playing video games, board games, or something else. Do you do this alone or with others? Describe this game and why you enjoy it so much.

Use the space below to draw a picture of yourself playing your favorite game.

ALL ABOUT ME

What are you good at? Drawing? Dancing? Singing? Or maybe it's playing an instrument or a sport. Write about this hobby, how you got started, and why you enjoy it.

_____

_____

_____

_____

_____

_____

_____

_____

_____

_____

_____

_____

_____

_____

_____

_____

_____

_____

_____

_____

_____

ALL ABOUT ME

Write about your favorite TV show. Is it a cartoon? A comedy, mystery, or something else? Describe the show and your favorite character in it.

_____

_____

_____

_____

_____

_____

_____

_____

_____

_____

_____

_____

_____

_____

_____

_____

_____

_____

_____

_____

_____

ALL ABOUT ME

Think about your all-time best birthday. How old were you? Did you have a party or go somewhere special? Did you receive a unique gift? Write about this amazing birthday and who shared it with you.

_____

_____

_____

_____

_____

_____

_____

_____

_____

_____

_____

_____

_____

_____

_____

_____

_____

_____

_____

_____

_____

_____

ALL ABOUT ME

Almost everyone loves summer. Think about some things you do during that season. Do you take trips? Visit relatives? Go to the pool or the beach? What are your favorite things about summer?

(If you are not a fan of summer, pick another season and tell what you like about it.)

_____

_____

_____

_____

_____

_____

_____

_____

_____

_____

_____

_____

_____

_____

_____

_____

_____

_____

_____

_____

_____

ALL ABOUT ME

What is something you are afraid of? Spiders? Snakes? Thunder-storms? Being home alone?

Write about this fear and how you deal with it.

_____
_____
_____
_____
_____
_____
_____
_____
_____
_____
_____
_____
_____
_____
_____
_____
_____
_____
_____
_____
_____

ALL ABOUT ME

Most people like collecting things such as coins, seashells, toys, Pokemon cards, stuffed animals, etc. What do you like to collect? How long have you been collecting these things? How many do you have?

Use the space below to draw something you collect, then write about your collection.

_____

_____

_____

_____

_____

_____

_____

_____

_____

_____

_____

ALL ABOUT ME

What is something you are proud of? Is it something you accomplished at school? Was it a goal you achieved? Or maybe an act of kindness toward another person. Tell us what you did and why it made you feel proud.

_____

_____

_____

_____

_____

_____

_____

_____

_____

_____

_____

_____

_____

_____

_____

_____

_____

_____

_____

_____

FRIENDS & FAMILY

Write about a pet your family has. Is it a dog, a cat, or something else? What is its name? What does it like to do? Play? Sleep? Who takes care of it? If your family does not have a pet, tell us about a pet you'd like to have and why.

Use the space below to draw a picture of your pet or a pet you would like to have.

FRIENDS & FAMILY

Tell us about your family. Is it big or small? Who do you get along with the best? Which family member do you spend the most time with? Why?

FRIENDS & FAMILY

Think about your best friend (no name required). How long have you known them? How or where did you meet? Describe why this person is such a good friend.

_____
_____
_____
_____
_____
_____
_____
_____
_____
_____
_____
_____
_____
_____
_____
_____
_____
_____
_____

BFF

FRIENDS & FAMILY

Write about a time you got in trouble at home. What did you do? What happened as a result? Describe what you learned from this experience.

_____

_____

_____

_____

_____

_____

_____

_____

_____

_____

_____

_____

_____

_____

_____

_____

_____

_____

_____

_____

FRIENDS & FAMILY

Where would you go if you could take a trip or vacation with your family? Disney World? Six Flags? The Grand Canyon? Somewhere else? Describe what you see and do on this trip.

_____

_____

_____

_____

_____

_____

_____

_____

_____

_____

_____

_____

_____

FRIENDS & FAMILY

Who is the funniest person in your family? Why? Do they tell jokes?
Play pranks? Do they act silly? Describe what this person does that
keeps you smiling and laughing.

_____

_____

_____

_____

_____

_____

_____

_____

_____

_____

_____

_____

_____

_____

_____

_____

_____

_____

FRIENDS & FAMILY

Imagine you're having a sleepover at your house. Describe your night of fun. Who are you going to invite? What foods or snacks will you have? Will you play games? Watch movies? How late will you stay up?

_____

_____

_____

_____

_____

_____

_____

_____

_____

_____

_____

_____

_____

_____

_____

_____

_____

_____

_____

BFF

FRIENDS & FAMILY

Someone in your family is having a birthday! Using markers, glue, scissors, etc., you make a special card for them. Who is the card for? Describe how you decorate it. What message do you write on the inside?

Use the template below to design your card.

Front	Inside

_____

_____

_____

_____

_____

_____

_____

_____

_____

FRIENDS & FAMILY

Compare yourself with your best friend. How are you alike? How are you different? Do you like the same music, movies, and books? Do you eat different foods? Name at least one thing about your friend that you admire.

_____

_____

_____

_____

_____

_____

_____

_____

_____

_____

_____

_____

_____

_____

_____

_____

_____

_____

_____

_____

_____

FRIENDS & FAMILY

Your family is planning a picnic. Where should it be? The park? The beach? Your backyard? Write about the location, food, and games everyone will enjoy at your picnic. Include who you will invite. Is it just for your family, or will you also invite friends, neighbors, or other relatives?

_____

_____

_____

_____

_____

_____

_____

_____

_____

_____

_____

_____

_____

WOULD YOU RATHER?

Would you rather spend a day at the zoo or an amusement park? Explain your choice and describe what you see and do while you're there.

_____

_____

_____

_____

_____

_____

_____

_____

_____

_____

_____

_____

_____

_____

_____

WOULD YOU RATHER?

Would you rather have a bird or a mouse as a pet? Explain your choice and describe how you would take care of your pet.

_____
_____
_____
_____
_____
_____
_____
_____
_____
_____
_____
_____
_____
_____
_____
_____
_____
_____
_____
_____

WOULD YOU RATHER?

Would you rather spend a night camping with your family or a day at the pool with them? Which would be more fun? Explain what you would do.

_____

_____

_____

_____

_____

_____

_____

_____

_____

_____

_____

_____

_____

_____

_____

_____

_____

_____

_____

_____

WOULD YOU RATHER?

Would you rather have a pet dragon or a pet unicorn? Where would you keep this pet? What would you feed it? What things would you do with your amazing pet?

   Use the space below to draw a picture of this unusual pet.

WOULD YOU RATHER?

Would you rather spend an entire day in the library or a tree house? Why? What will you do all day in that place?

_____

_____

_____

_____

_____

_____

_____

_____

_____

_____

_____

_____

_____

WOULD YOU RATHER?

Would you rather meet your favorite athlete or your favorite pop star? Why is this person your favorite? What things would you do and talk about with them?

_____

_____

_____

_____

_____

_____

_____

_____

_____

_____

_____

_____

_____

_____

_____

_____

_____

_____

_____

_____

WOULD YOU RATHER?

Would you rather go to school for six weeks in the summer or spend six weeks living and working on a farm? Which sounds easier? Which sounds like more fun? Explain your choice and what a typical day might look like.

_____

_____

_____

_____

_____

_____

_____

_____

_____

_____

_____

_____

_____

_____

_____

_____

_____

_____

_____

_____

_____

WOULD YOU RATHER?

Would you rather wear Crocs or sneakers? Explain why you chose that footwear and not the other.

Using the space below, draw a picture of your favorite shoes.

WOULD YOU RATHER?

Would you rather shave your head or dye your hair purple? Explain why you made that choice. What will your friends say when they see your new look?

Draw a "before" and "after" picture of your hairstyle.

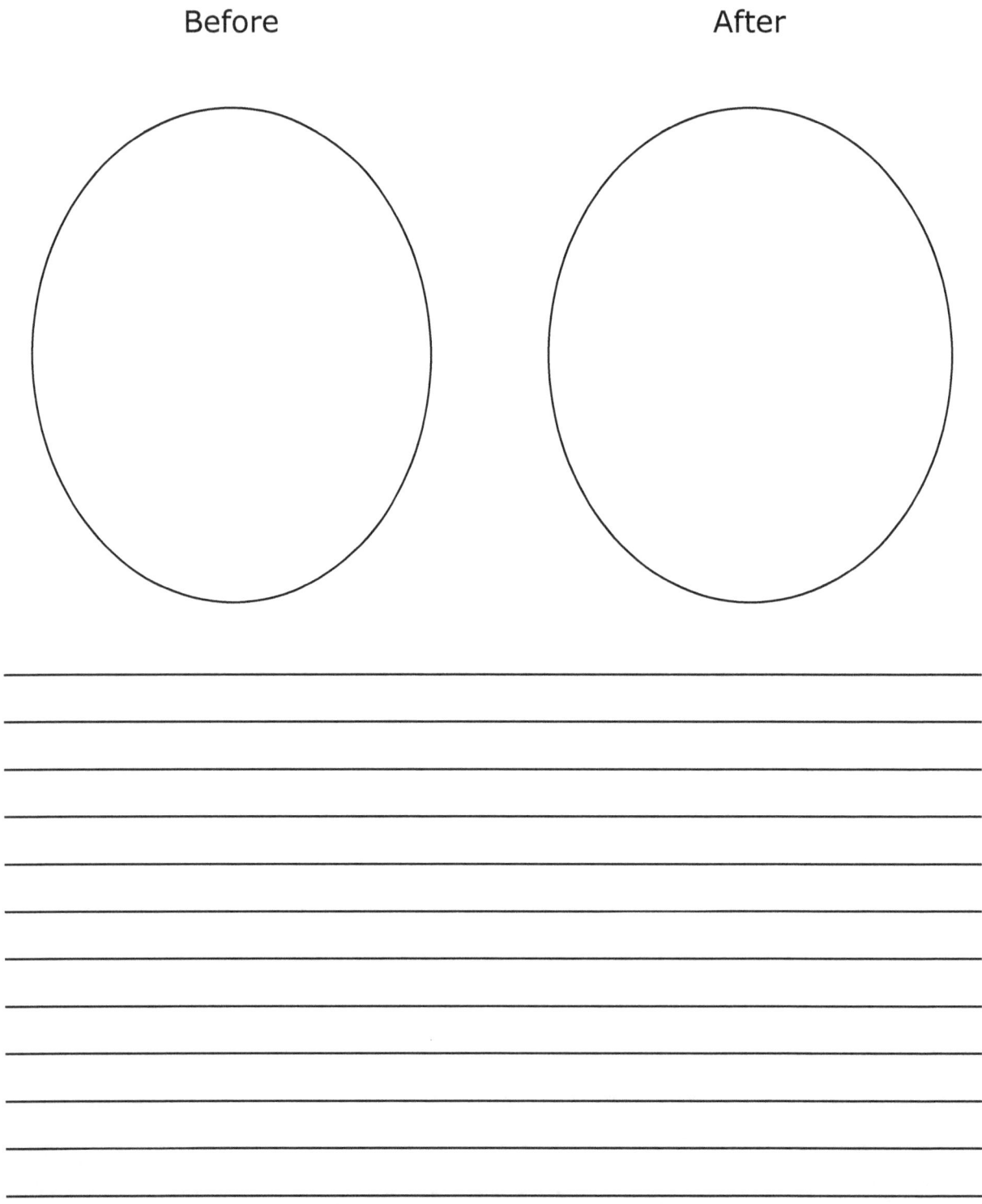

Before   After

_____

_____

_____

_____

_____

_____

_____

_____

_____

_____

_____

WOULD YOU RATHER?

Would you rather go a week without a shower or a week without TV? Which would be more difficult? What do your parents think of your choice?

_____

_____

_____

_____

_____

_____

_____

_____

_____

_____

_____

_____

_____

_____

_____

_____

_____

_____

_____

_____

WHAT IN THE WORLD?

Imagine you lived in prehistoric times when dinosaurs roamed the earth. One day, you see a T-Rex chasing another creature.

Describe the T-Rex and its prey. Does the animal escape or not? Write about what happens.

WHAT IN THE WORLD?

You think your neighbor might be a vampire or werewolf. One night, he walks out of his house, and you follow him. Where does he go? What does he do? Describe what happens.

WHAT IN THE WORLD?

A strange spaceship lands in your backyard one night. Slowly, the spaceship's door opens, and three aliens come out! What do they look like? What do they do next?

Use the space below to draw a picture of the spaceship and aliens.

_____

_____

_____

_____

_____

_____

_____

_____

_____

_____

_____

WHAT IN THE WORLD?

One day, you find a strange-looking lamp under an old tree. When you touch the lamp, a genie appears and grants you three wishes. What things do you wish for? What happens after each wish comes true?

_____
_____
_____
_____
_____
_____
_____
_____
_____
_____
_____
_____
_____
_____
_____
_____
_____
_____
_____
_____
_____

WHAT IN THE WORLD?

On the way home from school, you notice a dog you have never seen before following you. When you turn and say something to the dog, it talks back to you! Do you take the dog home with you? Why or why not? Describe what happens the rest of the day.

_____

_____

_____

_____

_____

_____

_____

_____

_____

_____

_____

WHAT IN THE WORLD?

One morning, you show up at school, and all the adults are missing. No teachers, principal, or staff. What happened? Did they all quit? Did aliens abduct them? Are they playing a prank? Describe the rest of the school day.

WHAT IN THE WORLD?

The new kid at school comes to your house and tells you he is a wizard with magical powers. You say you don't believe him, and he says, "Watch this."

Describe what happens next and what you and your new friend do the rest of the day.

WHAT IN THE WORLD?

One night, you dream you can fly. The next day, you realize your dream came true. That night after dark, you go outside. Where do you fly to? What do you see? Will you tell anyone about your new ability? Explain.

_____

_____

_____

_____

_____

_____

_____

_____

_____

_____

_____

_____

_____

_____

_____

_____

_____

WHAT IN THE WORLD?

You're at the beach when an old bottle with a piece of paper inside floats onto the shore. You open the bottle and look at the paper. What is it? A letter? A treasure map? Something in an unknown language? Describe what you found on the paper and what happens next.

Draw a picture of what you found on the paper.

_____

_____

_____

_____

_____

_____

_____

_____

_____

_____

WHAT IN THE WORLD?

While playing video games late one night, you get a strange message. Another player claims she is from the future—the year 2060! At first, you think it's a joke, but then the player tells you about life in 2060.

What things does she tell you? Do you believe her? What happens next?

_____

_____

_____

_____

_____

_____

_____

_____

_____

_____

_____

_____

_____

_____

_____

_____

_____

_____

_____

_____

AMAZING ADVENTURES

Your spaceship is on a journey to study Mars when you see three mysterious objects flying next to you! Describe the size, shape, and color of these strange objects. How do they behave? What happens next?

_____

_____

_____

_____

_____

_____

_____

_____

_____

_____

_____

_____

_____

_____

_____

_____

AMAZING ADVENTURES

You are in a thick jungle with a small team of explorers when you hear a large animal slowly approaching you. What kind of animal is it? Describe what happens next.

_____

_____

_____

_____

_____

_____

_____

_____

_____

_____

_____

_____

_____

_____

_____

_____

_____

_____

_____

_____

_____

AMAZING ADVENTURES

You are with a parent on a cross-country road trip to visit your grandparents. It will take you a week or two to reach your destination.

Describe what happens along the way. Where do you stop to eat and sleep? What things do you see on your trip? Does anything delay your journey (car trouble, animal sightings, detours, etc.)?

_____

_____

_____

_____

_____

_____

_____

_____

_____

_____

_____

_____

_____

_____

_____

_____

_____

_____

_____

_____

_____

AMAZING ADVENTURES

You are on a ship in the Pacific Ocean when a storm comes up. In the distance, you see a tiny island and go there for safety. What do you find on the island? People? Animals? A volcano? What happens next? What happens next?

Use the space below to draw a picture of what you see on the island.

AMAZING ADVENTURES

One afternoon, your school bus is heading down the road when you hear sirens. Looking out the window, you see five police cars with their lights flashing following the bus! Describe what happens next.

_____

_____

_____

_____

_____

_____

_____

_____

_____

_____

_____

_____

_____

_____

AMAZING ADVENTURES

You and your friends are camping in the mountains. In the middle of the night, you discover someone from your group is missing!

What do you and the other campers do? Do you leave camp and look for your friend? Do you wait to see if they return? What happens next?

_____

_____

_____

_____

_____

_____

_____

_____

_____

_____

_____

_____

_____

_____

_____

_____

_____

_____

_____

_____

AMAZING ADVENTURES

One day, your grandfather comes to your house and says he needs your help. At first, you don't understand. Then he shows you a wrinkled piece of yellow paper—a treasure map!

Describe what happens next. Where is the treasure located? Do you and your grandfather find it? If so, what is inside the treasure chest?

_____

_____

_____

_____

_____

_____

_____

_____

_____

_____

_____

_____

_____

_____

_____

_____

_____

_____

_____

_____

AMAZING ADVENTURES

You are at the zoo on a field trip, but as you are about to leave, you hear shouts, screams, and laughter. Dozens of monkeys and chimpanzees have escaped their enclosures. They jump on the bus, and some even get inside. What happens next?

Use the space below to draw a picture of the bus and the monkeys.

AMAZING ADVENTURES

Your team is playing the first game of the season. What sport are you playing, and how do you feel as you ride to the game?

   Describe what happens at the game. How do you play? Does your team win?

_____

_____

_____

_____

_____

_____

_____

_____

_____

_____

_____

_____

_____

_____

_____

_____

_____

AMAZING ADVENTURES

You take your family's canoe for a quick trip across the lake but get lost. What happens next? Do you try to find your way back? Does someone help you? How do you get home?

_____

_____

_____

_____

_____

_____

_____

_____

_____

_____

_____

_____

_____

_____

_____

_____

_____

_____

_____

_____

_____

BIG DREAMS

Imagine you have designed a new video game that makes you millions of dollars.

    Describe the game you created. What is it about? How do you play it? Next, describe your new life as a famous inventor and millionaire.

_____

_____

_____

_____

_____

_____

_____

_____

_____

_____

_____

_____

_____

_____

_____

_____

_____

_____

_____

_____

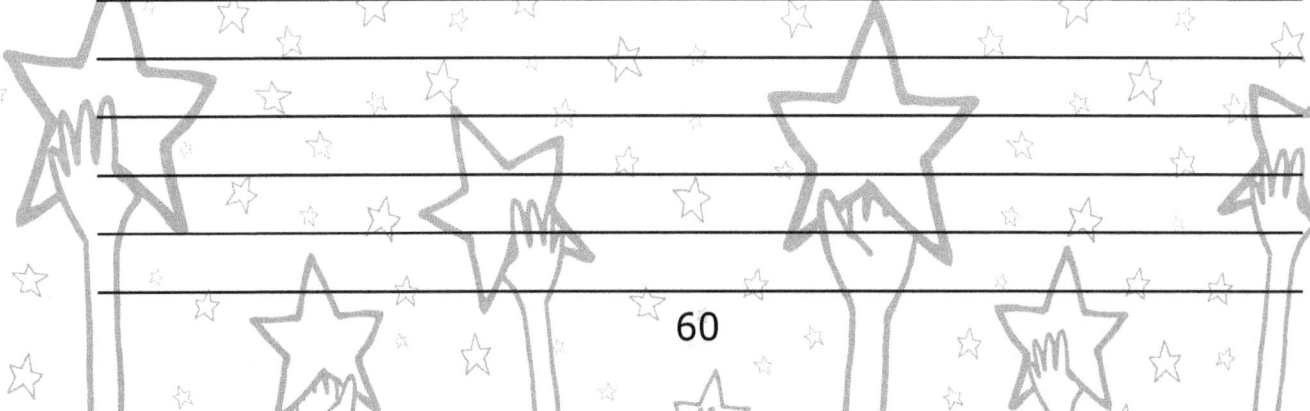

BIG DREAMS

You win a contest, and the prize is two plane tickets to anywhere in the world. Where are you going? Who are you taking with you? Describe the things you will see and do.

_____

_____

_____

_____

_____

_____

_____

_____

_____

_____

_____

_____

_____

_____

_____

_____

_____

_____

_____

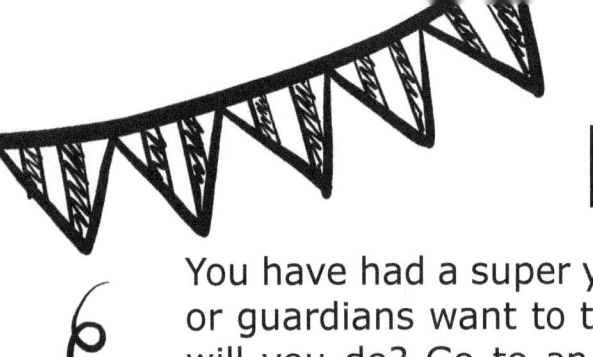

BIG DREAMS

You have had a super year and did great at school, so your parents or guardians want to throw you a party. Who do you invite? What will you do? Go to an amusement park? Have a big party in the backyard? Invite friends for a sleepover and stay up all night?

_____

_____

_____

_____

_____

_____

_____

_____

_____

_____

_____

_____

_____

_____

_____

_____

_____

_____

_____

_____

_____

BIG DREAMS

You get to go into space on a special mission. What do you do during your mission? What do you see and learn during your time in outer space?

_____

_____

_____

_____

_____

_____

_____

_____

_____

_____

_____

_____

_____

_____

_____

_____

_____

_____

_____

BIG DREAMS

A crew is making a movie in your town, and you get to be in it. What kind of movie is it? Adventure? Horror? Comedy? Tell us about the movie and the role you play.

Use the template to design a poster for the movie.

BIG DREAMS

A helicopter is waiting for you and your best friend after school. Who sent the helicopter? Where does it take you? Who do you meet on this mysterious adventure?

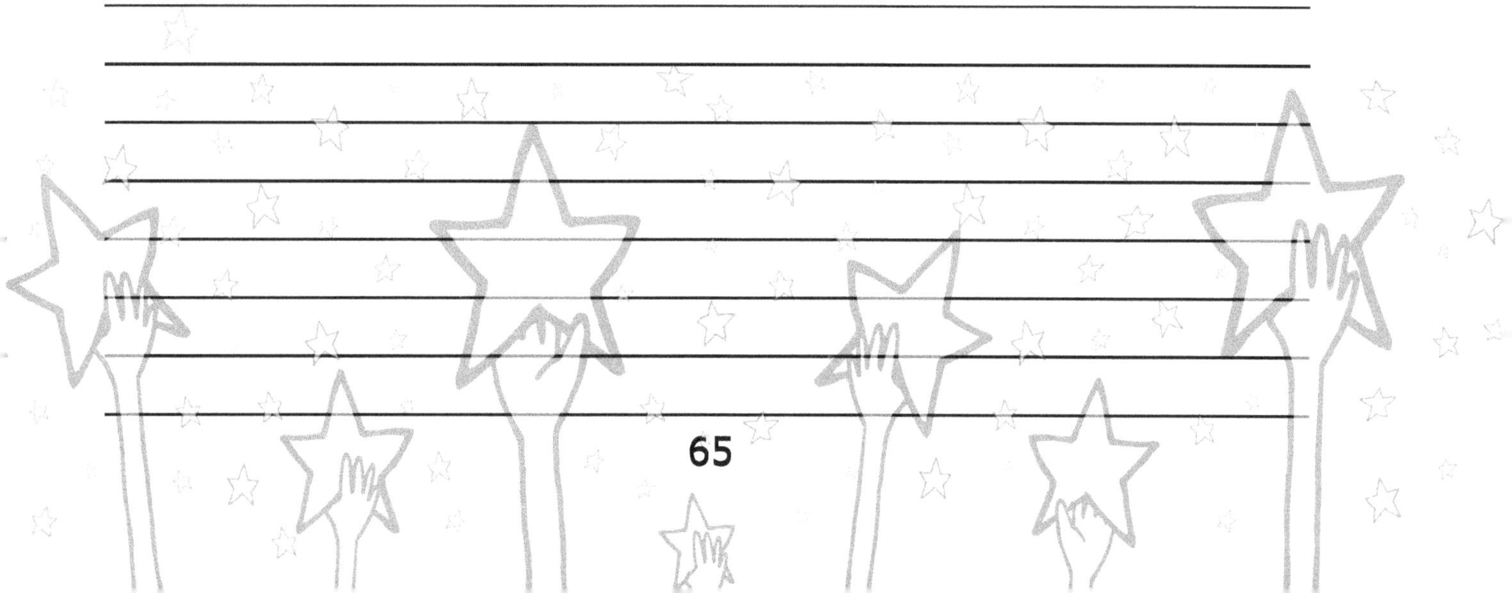

_____

_____

_____

_____

_____

_____

_____

_____

_____

_____

_____

_____

_____

_____

_____

_____

_____

_____

_____

_____

BIG DREAMS

Imagine that, for one day, you are a superhero. What do you call yourself? What is your superpower, and what can you do with it? How do people react to you?

_____

_____

_____

_____

_____

_____

_____

_____

_____

_____

_____

_____

_____

_____

_____

_____

_____

_____

_____

_____

BIG DREAMS

What would be your dream job? Veterinarian? Pro athlete? Pop star?

Explain why that job would be perfect for you. Describe what you might do on a typical day.

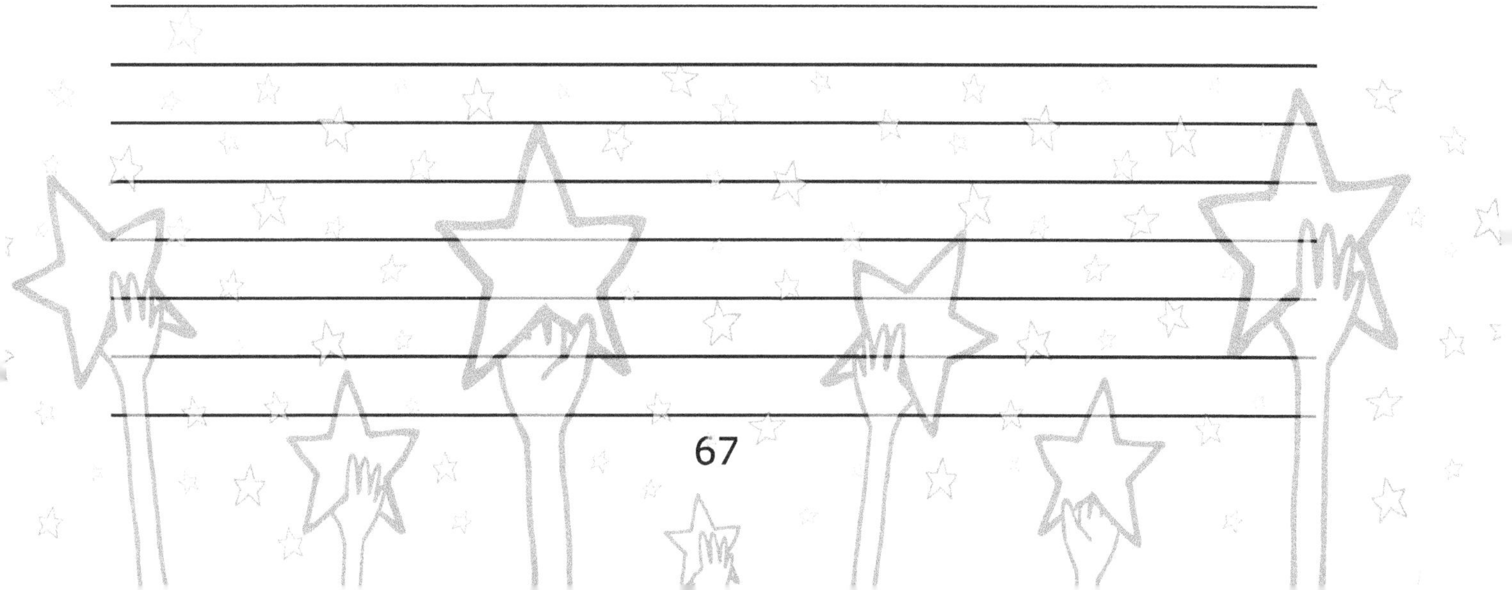

_____

_____

_____

_____

_____

_____

_____

_____

_____

_____

_____

_____

_____

_____

_____

_____

_____

_____

_____

BIG DREAMS

Imagine scientists have discovered a small island that still has dinosaurs living on it. You and a few classmates get to visit the island. You will take photos and keep a journal, which you will share with your school and local TV station.

Write your first journal entry describing the island and creatures you see. Use the space to draw a picture of one of the dinosaurs.

BIG DREAMS

After months of hard work, you have invented a time machine. Now, you have the chance to use it. What will you do? Will you go back in time or into the future? Tell us what you see and do on your trip.

_____

_____

_____

_____

_____

_____

_____

_____

_____

_____

_____

TELL ME A STORY

"What's that noise?" whispers your friend, Chris. The tent is dark, and you can hear rustling nearby. It sounds like a large animal is in your campsite!

What do you do? What is making the noise? Describe what you see and do when you look outside the tent.

_____

_____

_____

_____

_____

_____

_____

_____

_____

_____

_____

_____

_____

_____

_____

_____

_____

_____

TELL ME A STORY

Your rowboat drifts further and further away from the lakeshore. You try rowing back to shore, but the wind is too strong.

What happens to you? How long are you stranded in the boat? Do you get rescued? If so, by whom?

_____

_____

_____

_____

_____

_____

_____

_____

_____

_____

_____

_____

_____

TELL ME A STORY

As you walk home from school, an old car pulls up beside you. A classmate leans out the window.

"Can you help me?"

What type of help does your friend want? Do you decide to help her? What happens next? Maybe end the story with something funny.

_____

_____

_____

_____

_____

_____

_____

_____

_____

_____

_____

_____

_____

_____

_____

_____

_____

_____

_____

_____

TELL ME A STORY

A classmate runs up to you in the hallway. He is nearly out of breath. "Did you hear what happened in Mr. Perry's class today?"

Write about what happened in Mr. Perry's room. Was it funny, scary, or embarrassing?

_____

_____

_____

_____

_____

_____

_____

_____

_____

_____

_____

_____

_____

_____

_____

_____

_____

_____

_____

_____

_____

_____

TELL ME A STORY

Something catches your eye while you walk through the woods. It's a young deer hiding behind a tree. You look for its mother, but no other deer is in sight. Do you stay by the fawn or leave to find help? Does its mother come back?

Use the space below to draw a picture of the deer.

TELL ME A STORY

Your team is down by one point when your teammate Jess comes over and whispers a play in your ear. It sounds like a great idea, but will it work?

What does Jess say? Describe the play and how the game ends.

TELL ME A STORY

A blinding red light shines through your bedroom window, waking you up. You look at the clock on your nightstand. It's nearly 3:00 AM. Suddenly, the ground begins to shake. Getting out of bed, you look outside and can't believe your eyes.

What do you see in the backyard? What does it do? Describe what happens next.

Use the space below to draw a picture of what you see.

TELL ME A STORY

Dad walks into your room with a big grin on his face. "Look what I have," he says, holding up two tickets.

Where are you and your dad going? To a concert or sporting event? Something else? Describe what happens at the event.

Decorate the blank ticket below, and include the name of the event.

_____

_____

_____

_____

_____

_____

_____

_____

_____

_____

_____

TELL ME A STORY

You never believed in ghosts — until now. On Halloween night, you stand beside your two best friends in the old Grimson mansion. Suddenly, you see something move.

Why are you in the old house? Whose idea was it? Are there ghosts there, or is it a prank?

_____

_____

_____

_____

_____

_____

_____

_____

_____

_____

_____

_____

_____

_____

_____

_____

_____

_____

_____

_____

TELL ME A STORY

Your sister doesn't play jokes or pranks, so you get nervous when she enters the room with a serious expression on her face.

"Look at this," she says, holding out her hand.

What is in her hand? Something gross? Weird? Valuable? Explain what she does with the object.

_____

_____

_____

_____

_____

_____

_____

_____

_____

_____

_____

_____

_____

_____

_____

_____

_____

_____

_____

_____

_____

_____

IN MY OPINION

Pizza is better than chicken nuggets. Do you agree or disagree? Choose which food you like better and tell us why it's the best. Do you make it at home or buy it from a restaurant?

Give your opinion and tell us your favorite place to get this meal.

IN MY OPINION

Dogs are better pets than cats. Do you agree or disagree?
Describe which one is a better pet and explain your choice. What are the pros and cons of each animal?

_____

_____

_____

_____

_____

_____

_____

_____

_____

_____

_____

_____

IN MY OPINION

Kids should be able to go to bed when they want. Do you agree or disagree?

Most parents set a bedtime for their children, but some don't. Do you think a scheduled bedtime is a good thing? Why or why not?

What time should kids go to bed? 8:00 PM? 9:00 PM? Later? Give reasons for your answer.

_____

_____

_____

_____

_____

_____

_____

_____

_____

_____

_____

_____

_____

_____

_____

_____

_____

_____

_____

IN MY OPINION

Ice cream is the best dessert ever. Do you agree? If not, what dessert do you think is best? Cookies? Cupcakes? Brownies? Something else?

Write about your favorite dessert and why you think it's the best. Use the space to draw a picture of the best dessert ever.

IN MY OPINION

There are too many tests at school. Do you agree or disagree? Do tests help you? In what ways are tests useful for you or your teachers? In what ways are they not?

_____

_____

_____

_____

_____

_____

_____

_____

_____

_____

_____

_____

_____

_____

_____

_____

_____

_____

_____

_____

IN MY OPINION

Special classes like art, music, and PE are the most fun and interesting. Do you agree or disagree?

Are special classes your favorites, or do you prefer classes like Math and ELA (Language Arts)? Which class is your favorite? Why?

_____

_____

_____

_____

_____

_____

_____

_____

_____

_____

_____

_____

_____

_____

_____

_____

_____

_____

_____

_____

IN MY OPINION

Warm states like Florida, Texas, and Arizona are the best places to live. Do you agree, or do you like cooler climates? Explain your answer and include activities you can do in that climate.

Draw a picture of one of these activities.

IN MY OPINION

Kids should be able to choose what they want to eat. Do you agree or disagree? If kids can choose their own food, will they make healthy choices? How can kids and parents agree on food choices?

_____

_____

_____

_____

_____

_____

_____

_____

_____

_____

_____

_____

_____

_____

_____

_____

_____

_____

_____

IN MY OPINION

Kids should be able to play whatever video games they want. Do you agree or disagree?

Are some games too scary, violent, or inappropriate for kids? How do you decide which games are okay and which are not?

_____
_____
_____
_____
_____
_____
_____
_____
_____
_____
_____

IN MY OPINION

Today's cartoons are better than the old ones your parents watched when they were kids. Do you agree or disagree?

Discuss which cartoons you like more and why you think they are better. Which one is your favorite? Why?

_____

_____

_____

_____

_____

_____

_____

_____

_____

_____

_____

_____

_____

_____

_____

_____

_____

_____

_____

_____

_____

WHAT WOULD YOU DO?

What would you do if your parent got a new job and you had to move? How would you feel? What would you tell your friends? What things would you do together before you moved? How would you stay in touch with your friends?

_____
_____
_____
_____
_____
_____
_____
_____
_____
_____
_____
_____
_____
_____
_____
_____
_____
_____
_____
_____
_____

WHAT WOULD YOU DO?

What would you do if a big snowstorm trapped you inside a store overnight? Would you be excited or frightened? Would you play with the toys and games? Go shopping? What would you eat?

_____
_____
_____
_____
_____
_____
_____
_____
_____
_____
_____
_____
_____
_____
_____
_____
_____
_____
_____
_____
_____

WHAT WOULD YOU DO?

What would you do if you saw a neighbor kid sneaking around your backyard? Would you talk to them? Tell your parents what you saw? Describe what happens and what you discover.

_____

_____

_____

_____

_____

_____

_____

_____

_____

_____

_____

WHAT WOULD YOU DO?

What would you do if you spilled something on the carpet? Would you clean it up? Would you keep quiet or tell your parents? Explain your decision.

_____

_____

_____

_____

_____

_____

_____

_____

_____

_____

_____

_____

_____

_____

_____

_____

_____

_____

_____

_____

_____

WHAT WOULD YOU DO?

What would you do if your best friend was in the hospital? Would you call them? Visit them? Make them a card? What could you say and do to help your friend feel better?

_____

_____

_____

_____

_____

_____

_____

_____

_____

_____

_____

_____

_____

_____

_____

_____

_____

_____

_____

_____

_____

WHAT WOULD YOU DO?

What would you do all summer if there were no rules? Would you sleep late? Watch movies all day? Go to the pool? Ride your bike across town? Eat whatever you want? Describe what you do during your summer of freedom.

_____

_____

_____

_____

_____

_____

_____

_____

_____

_____

_____

_____

_____

_____

_____

_____

_____

_____

_____

_____

WHAT WOULD YOU DO?

What would you do if you saw a ghost? Would it scare you? Who would you tell? Would you ever return to the place you saw it?

Use the space below to draw a picture of the ghost and describe how you would react to it.

WHAT WOULD YOU DO?

What would you do if you saw a student take something from someone else's backpack? Would you talk to the thief? What would you say? Would you tell a friend, teacher, or counselor? What consequence do you think the student should receive?

_____

_____

_____

_____

_____

_____

_____

_____

_____

_____

_____

_____

_____

_____

_____

_____

_____

_____

_____

_____

WHAT WOULD YOU DO?

What would you do if the toys in your room all came to life? Would you stay quiet and watch them? Talk to them? Run and tell your parents? Are you frightened or excited about the toys coming to life?

Use the space below to draw a picture of your toys coming to life.

WHAT WOULD YOU DO?

What if your hair grew several inches every day? Would you cut it each day? Experiment with different hair styles? Dye it different colors? Shave your head every few weeks? Grow it out and donate it?

Describe what you would do with your fast-growing hair.

_____

_____

_____

_____

_____

_____

_____

_____

_____

_____

_____

_____

CHOICES & CHALLENGES

Someone at school is bullying you. How does it make you feel? Who do you tell? A teacher, friend, or parent? What consequences should the bully face?

_____

_____

_____

_____

_____

_____

_____

_____

_____

_____

_____

_____

_____

_____

_____

_____

_____

CHOICES & CHALLENGES

A friend invites you to a party but also invites someone you don't get along with. Should you go to the party or stay home? Why?
    If you attend the party, will you avoid the person you dislike or try to get to know them better?

_____
_____
_____
_____
_____
_____
_____
_____
_____
_____
_____
_____
_____
_____
_____
_____
_____
_____
_____
_____

CHOICES & CHALLENGES

Your friend tells you a secret and asks you not to share it with anyone, but you're unsure what to do. What kind of secret is this? Should you tell an adult?

When is it okay to keep a secret, and when should you share it?

_____

_____

_____

_____

_____

_____

_____

_____

_____

_____

_____

CHOICES & CHALLENGES

Your parents ask you to finish your homework before playing video games or going out to play. But a friend stops by and asks you to hang out. What do you do? What do you say to your friend?

_____

_____

_____

_____

_____

_____

_____

_____

_____

_____

_____

_____

_____

_____

_____

_____

_____

_____

_____

CHOICES & CHALLENGES

You and your best friend argued at recess and are not speaking to each other.

How do you fix the problem? Do you DM (Direct Message) them or talk to them in person? Do you apologize or wait for their apology? What do you say once you are talking to each other again?

_____

_____

_____

_____

_____

_____

_____

_____

_____

_____

_____

_____

_____

_____

_____

_____

_____

_____

_____

_____

CHOICES & CHALLENGES

You promise to take care of your new dog but watch a movie instead of feeding and walking it. When your parents ask about the dog, what do you tell them? How can you be more responsible in the future?

Use the space below to draw a picture of your dog.

CHOICES & CHALLENGES

You forgot to study for the weekly spelling quiz and feel anxious about taking it. What do you do? Try your best? Pretend to be sick? Try to cheat? What do you tell your teacher or parents after the test?

Write what you do in this situation and what happens because of your choice.

_____

_____

_____

_____

_____

_____

_____

_____

_____

_____

_____

_____

_____

_____

_____

_____

_____

_____

_____

_____

_____

_____

_____

CHOICES & CHALLENGES

While walking down the hall at school, you spot a $20 bill on the floor. What do you do? Keep the money? Tell a teacher? Describe what you do with the money and why you made that choice.

Using the space below, draw a picture showing what you would do with the money.

_____
_____
_____
_____
_____
_____
_____
_____
_____
_____
_____

CHOICES & CHALLENGES

Your brother or sister lies to your parents about something that happened in the neighborhood. However, you saw what happened and know the truth.

What did your brother or sister do? What do you say to your sibling? Do you tell your parents? Explain what you do.

_____

_____

_____

_____

_____

_____

_____

_____

_____

_____

_____

_____

_____

_____

_____

_____

_____

_____

_____

CHOICES & CHALLENGES

When was the last time you were very upset? Describe what happened. How did you deal with the situation? What did you learn?

_____

_____

_____

_____

_____

_____

_____

_____

_____

_____

_____

_____

_____

_____

_____

_____

_____

_____

_____

_____

CHOICES & CHALLENGES

You are in the store with your parents and see something you want. It's not very expensive, so you ask your parents if they will buy it for you, but they say "No."

You're upset. The more you think about it, the more you want the item. What do you do? What should you do? Save up your money to buy it yourself? Steal it? Forget about it? Why did you make that choice?

_____

_____

_____

_____

_____

_____

_____

_____

_____

_____

_____

_____

_____

_____

_____

_____

_____

_____

_____

ABOUT THE AUTHOR

MARK TREVOR has been a language arts teacher for nearly 25 years and has taught students from kindergarten through grade 12. He currently lives in Cary, North Carolina.